AF779372

Table Of Contents

Preface

The world of product management has never been more exciting or more perilous. In the last two decades, we have witnessed an extraordinary acceleration in the creation of digital products that power every part of our daily lives. From the mobile applications we depend on for banking and healthcare to the platforms that manage supply chains and critical infrastructure, products are no longer simple tools; they are the very scaffolding of modern society. With this centrality comes responsibility, and with responsibility comes risk.

When I first began leading product-focused initiatives in cybersecurity, the conversations in boardrooms and design meetings centered almost exclusively around features, usability, and market fit. Cybersecurity was acknowledged, but often considered someone else's problem, the domain of security engineers, compliance officers, or IT departments. Product teams were rarely asked to think deeply about resilience, nor were they empowered to influence it. The prevailing assumption was that as long as security protocols were in place, resilience would take care of itself.

That assumption has proven dangerously inadequate. High-profile breaches, catastrophic ransomware attacks, and global disruptions have taught us that resilience is not an afterthought;

it is a design principle, a cultural mindset, and a competitive differentiator. Products that fail to anticipate and withstand attacks lose not only revenue but trust, an intangible asset that, once broken, is almost impossible to restore. Customers may forgive a feature delay or a design misstep, but they rarely forgive the compromise of their data, their privacy, or their confidence.

This book was born out of my conviction that product managers cannot afford to remain on the sidelines of cybersecurity. We are the custodians of vision, the translators of strategy, and the advocates for users. If resilience is to be embedded into the DNA of digital products, it must begin with us. We must learn the language of risk, collaborate across disciplines, and make resilience as much a part of our thinking as customer journeys or feature prioritization.

The journey to writing this book has been shaped by countless interactions with professionals across Nigeria and the wider world; engineers, designers, regulators, entrepreneurs, and fellow product managers. I have seen startups unravel because they underestimated security from day one, and I have seen established enterprises scramble to retrofit resilience into systems that were never built to handle persistent threats. I have also seen inspiring examples of young innovators in Lagos, Ibadan, and Abuja who are proving that resilience can be designed into products from the ground up, even with limited resources. Their courage and ingenuity affirm my belief that cyber-resilience is not the privilege of large enterprises alone; it is a necessity for every builder in the digital economy.

As you read this book, you will encounter a structured journey: from understanding what cyber-resilience truly means, through embedding it into product strategy, to envisioning the future of resilient product management in an AI-driven world. Each chapter is designed to balance theory with practice, frameworks with case studies, and concepts with actionable insights. While I draw from global references, I remain intentional about highlighting African realities, because our contexts, challenges, and opportunities deserve visibility.

This is not a technical manual. You will not find pages of code snippets or encryption algorithms here. Instead, this book aims to equip you, the product manager, the strategist, the leader with the mindset and vocabulary you need to influence technical decisions, champion security with executives, and advocate resilience with customers. You will learn how to ask the right questions, frame the right trade-offs, and measure the right outcomes.

The decision to structure the book around ten chapters came from my desire to provide depth without overwhelming the reader. Each chapter tackles a distinct facet of cyber-resilience, from secure design to governance, from incident response to cross-functional collaboration. Together, they form a cohesive playbook that you can return to as your career evolves and as your products scale.

This book also carries a personal dimension. I grew up in an environment where resilience was not an abstract concept but a daily necessity. The Nigerian entrepreneurial spirit, marked by creativity, improvisation, and grit, taught me that survival and progress often depend on the ability to adapt under pressure. Translating that same spirit into the world of digital product management, I believe, is not only possible but essential. In many ways, cyber-resilience is simply the digital expression of what we, as Africans, have always known: strength lies not in avoiding storms but in withstanding and growing through them.

I invite you to approach this book not just as a guide but as a conversation. Some ideas will challenge your assumptions, others will affirm what you already practice, and still others may provoke you to rethink how your organization approaches resilience altogether. My hope is that by the time you close these pages, you will feel both equipped and inspired to lead the charge for cyber-resilient products in your own context.

Finally, I must acknowledge the people who made this work possible. My colleagues shared stories from the trenches of product crises. My mentors reminded me that resilience is as much about mindset as it is about systems. My students and peers who constantly pushed me to explain not just the "what" but the "why" behind resilient practices. And my family, whose patience and encouragement allowed me to spend long nights wrestling with drafts and revisions. To all of you, I am deeply grateful.

Cyber-resilience is not an endpoint; it is a journey. And every journey begins with a decision to take the first step. As you turn the page, I encourage you to see yourself not as a passive reader but as an active participant in shaping the future of safer, stronger, and more trusted digital products.

Foreword

In every era of innovation, there comes a defining moment when the creators of products must rethink their role. For the past decade, the conversation in product management has revolved around speed. how quickly we can design, iterate, and deliver. But today, speed without resilience is a liability. We are reminded, almost daily, that one cyber incident can wipe away years of progress, compromise millions of users, and erode trust faster than any competitor ever could.

This is why Adebayo Kalejaiye' s work in *A Product Manager's Guide to Building Cyber-Resilient Products* is so timely and necessary. He does not write as a theorist from the sidelines. He writes as a practitioner who has lived the tension between delivering features fast and ensuring that those features can withstand the pressures of a hostile digital environment. His voice is one that product managers in Lagos, London, or Los Angeles need to hear.

I first met Adebayo at a product roundtable in Abuja some years ago. The room was filled with discussions about design thinking, customer journeys, and market differentiation. But Adebayo asked the question that silenced the room: "What happens if our best-designed product is brought down by a single breach?" It was not a rhetorical flourish. It was a challenging reminder that in an interconnected world, resilience is not optional. That moment has stayed with me because it captured what this book now unpacks in detail: the need for product managers to own resilience as much as their own customer experience.

What sets this book apart is its clarity. Too often, discussions about cybersecurity are locked away in technical jargon, accessible only to engineers and compliance experts. Adebayo bridges that gap. He speaks directly to product managers, equipping them with the vocabulary, frameworks, and mindset needed to lead conversations about resilience at the highest levels. He reminds us that resilience is not just about defense; it is about foresight, collaboration, and adaptability.

Each chapter walks the reader through a critical dimension of resilience. From understanding the evolving threat landscape to embedding security in strategy, from cross-functional collaboration to incident management, the book provides a holistic approach that few texts achieve. For me, Chapter 8 on collaboration stands out. Too many organizations treat security as a silo, a department to consult only when compliance deadlines loom. Adebayo demonstrates that true resilience comes when product managers champion integration, breaking down silos and ensuring that design, engineering, marketing, and security move together toward a shared goal.

The African perspective woven throughout this book is also vital. Our continent is experiencing a digital renaissance, with startups emerging in fintech, healthtech, logistics, and more. Yet with this growth comes vulnerability. Cyberattacks on African firms have multiplied in recent years, targeting both the smallest innovators and the largest corporations. By grounding his analysis in both global frameworks and local realities, Adebayo provides a resource that speaks to the unique challenges and opportunities of building resilient products in contexts where resources are limited but ingenuity is abundant.

I also appreciate the human tone of this book. This is not a dry manual filled with checklists. It is a call to action. Adebayo speaks not only to the intellect but also to the conscience of product managers. He reminds us that every decision we make, how we store data, how we handle incidents, how we design defaults has real consequences for real people. In a world where trust is fragile, resilience is ultimately about protecting that trust.

To every product manager reading this, I encourage you to take this book seriously. Do not skim it as another industry text. Engage with it as a blueprint for how you will lead your own organization. Use it to spark conversations with your engineers, your executives, your regulators, and most importantly, your customers. Let it shape not just what you build but how you build.

Adebayo Kalejaiye has given us more than a guide. He has given us a lens through which to see the future of product management, one where resilience is not a cost center but a core value, not an afterthought but a differentiator. As cyber threats continue to evolve, this mindset will separate the products that endure from those that collapse under pressure.

I am honored to write this foreword, but more importantly, I am grateful that this book exists. It is a gift to the product management community, to African innovators, and to anyone who believes that technology should not only empower but also protect. May it inspire you, as it has inspired me, to build products that are not just useful or profitable but truly resilient.

Introduction

The twenty-first century has witnessed a dramatic shift in how products are conceived, built, and consumed. No longer are products confined to physical shelves or traditional markets. Today, every serious enterprise is also a digital enterprise, whether through a mobile application, a connected device, or a cloud-based service. Customers expect seamless access, fast updates, and continuous improvement. Yet beneath the surface of convenience lies a reality that many organizations overlook: digital products are exposed to threats that can destroy trust, disrupt services, and even put lives at risk.

Cyber-resilience has therefore emerged as one of the most critical attributes of successful products. Where cybersecurity emphasizes the protection of systems against attacks, cyber-resilience goes a step further. It is about ensuring that when, not if, an attack occurs, the product can withstand it, recover quickly, and continue to deliver value. Resilience is not about perfection. It is about continuity.

For too long, product managers have underestimated their role in this conversation. Security was considered a technical specialty; something left to engineers or IT departments. Product managers were taught to focus on features, user experience, and market opportunities. While these remain central, the assumption that resilience is someone else's problem is no longer sustainable. Customers do not distinguish between technical failure and product failure. If a breach disrupts access, corrupts data, or compromises privacy, the blame rests on the product, and by extension, the product manager.

Consider the recent wave of high-profile incidents that made global headlines. A major ride-hailing platform experienced a data breach that exposed millions of customer records. A payment startup lost credibility after a ransomware attack froze transactions for days. Even healthcare apps, designed to empower patients, have faced lawsuits when sensitive data leaked. In each case, the technical cause may have been buried in lines of code or flawed configurations, but the reputational damage was squarely a product problem.

This is where product managers must step forward. We are uniquely positioned to shape not only what products do, but how they are built. We sit at the intersection of strategy, design, and execution. We are translators between executives, engineers, and customers. If resilience is to be embedded into the DNA of products, it cannot be left to chance. It must be championed by those who oversee the product lifecycle from conception to retirement.

The purpose of this book is to equip product managers with the tools, frameworks, and mindset needed to make resilience a core part of product practice. It does not aim to turn product managers into security engineers. Instead, it helps them ask the right questions, frame the right trade-offs, and lead the right conversations. It positions resilience not as a constraint but as a differentiator. In competitive markets, the product that customers trust will outlast the one that merely dazzles with features.

The structure of this book reflects the holistic nature of resilience. The first chapters explore what cyber-resilience means and why it matters, setting a foundation of awareness. We then move into strategy, showing how resilience should be integrated into vision, roadmaps, and design. Technical aspects such as architecture, governance, and compliance are covered in ways that product managers can understand and influence, even if they are not coding themselves. Later chapters emphasize incident management, cross-functional collaboration, and metrics for measuring resilience. Finally, we look forward, exploring how trends such as artificial intelligence, automation, and quantum computing will shape the future of resilient products.

Throughout the book, real-world examples are used to ground theory in practice. While references are drawn from global incidents, attention is given to African contexts, where resources may be limited but creativity is abundant. In Nigeria, for instance, fintech startups have faced intense cyber threats even while building systems that bring millions of people into formal financial services for the first time. These stories remind us that resilience is not a luxury of large corporations. It is a survival requirement for every innovator.

Equally important is the cultural shift that resilience demands. Many organizations treat security as a checklist, an item to tick off for compliance purposes. True resilience requires a change in mindset. It requires product managers to champion security in design discussions, to prioritize customer trust as highly as revenue, and to see resilience as a shared responsibility across all teams. This book will show that leadership in resilience is not about technical mastery alone. It is about vision, influence, and persistence.

One theme you will notice is the balance between optimism and realism. On one hand, the threat landscape is daunting. Cybercriminals are organized, well-funded, and constantly innovating. On the other hand, resilience is achievable. With deliberate choices, strong collaboration, and clear priorities, product managers can build products that not only survive attacks but grow stronger from them. The key is to start early, act consistently, and never treat resilience as optional.

This introduction would be incomplete without a word on the human element. Behind every system, every breach, and every recovery are people. Users whose lives may be disrupted. Teams who must respond under pressure. Communities who depend on digital platforms for daily living. Resilience is ultimately about people. As you read, I encourage you to see beyond the technical concepts and frameworks. Think about the trust you hold in your hands as a product manager. Think about the responsibility to protect not only data but dignity.

It is also important to acknowledge that no single book can provide all the answers. Cyber-resilience is an evolving field, shaped by emerging threats and technologies. What this book offers is a foundation and a guide. It equips you with principles that endure even as tools and tactics change. It encourages you to keep learning, keep questioning, and keep adapting.

By the time you finish this book, you will not only understand resilience intellectually but also feel empowered to act on it. You will be able to map resilience into your product strategy, collaborate effectively with technical teams, and communicate the value of resilience to executives and stakeholders. Most importantly, you will see yourself as a leader in building a digital future that customers can trust.

Welcome to this journey. The road ahead will challenge your assumptions, stretch your skills, and sharpen your leadership. But it will also prepare you for a future where the products that thrive are the ones that endure. Cyber-resilience is not just the new frontier of product management. It is the foundation on which the next generation of trusted, transformative products will be built.

Chapter 1

Understanding Cyber-Resilience in the Product Lifecycle

When most people hear the word resilience, they think about strength in the face of adversity, the ability to recover after a setback, or the determination to keep moving despite challenges. In many ways, these same qualities apply to digital products. Just as individuals must endure pressure without breaking, products must withstand attacks, disruptions, and failures without collapsing. Cyber-resilience captures this principle in the digital age: it is the measure of a product's ability not just to avoid threats, but to absorb, recover, and continue functioning when threats inevitably occur.

To understand why this matters so much in product management, it is necessary to first step back and consider the nature of modern digital products. Products are no longer isolated creations, built once and delivered in a finished form. They are living systems, constantly updated, integrated with third-party services, connected to vast networks, and dependent on cloud infrastructure. A ride-hailing application, for instance, depends not only on its own codebase but also on payment processors, mapping services, telecom infrastructure, and user devices. Anyone of these elements can become a point of vulnerability.

The traditional model of product success has revolved around the product lifecycle: conception, design, development, launch, growth, maturity, and eventual decline or renewal. In each stage, product managers play a central role in defining priorities, allocating resources, and ensuring that customer value is delivered. Yet in most product lifecycles, resilience is rarely considered explicitly. Market research will analyze customer demand, competitive positioning, and pricing strategies, but it will often leave out questions such as: "What happens if our system is attacked?" or "How quickly can we recover from a breach without losing trust?" These omissions can be fatal.

Cyber-resilience must therefore be woven into every stage of the lifecycle. At the conception stage, when teams are brainstorming features, resilience should shape how problems are framed. Instead of asking only what customers want, product managers should also ask what customers fear losing; privacy, continuity, and trust. At the design stage, resilience should influence architecture decisions, user flows, and even the choice of default settings. During development, resilience should guide priorities such as secure coding practices, regular testing, and vulnerability assessments. At launch, resilience should inform how monitoring is established and how incident response plans are communicated. And in growth and maturity, resilience should be measured, refined, and improved as the product scales.

Consider an example from the Nigerian fintech ecosystem. A young startup launches an app that enables small traders to accept digital payments. The product gains traction quickly because it solves a real problem in the market. However, in the rush to acquire users, the team neglects to implement strong encryption for stored customer data. A few months later, a breach exposes thousands of transaction histories. Traders lose trust, customers abandon the app, and regulators intervene. The startup collapses, not because the idea was bad, but because resilience was never integrated into the lifecycle. The tragedy here is that resilience could have been achieved with relatively modest effort had it been prioritized early.

This is not to suggest that resilience is about building impenetrable systems. No such system exists. Cyber-resilience is instead about preparedness and adaptability. A resilient product anticipates that incidents will occur and builds pathways for recovery. It has redundancies in place, clear communication strategies, and a culture of learning from failures. Just as a resilient person may stumble but never stays down, a resilient product may falter under attack but regains its footing quickly, minimizing damage to users and the business.

One of the most important shifts for product managers is to see resilience as part of customer value. Customers rarely ask for encryption or incident response playbooks when filling out surveys. They ask for convenience, speed, and features. Yet beneath those expectations is an unspoken assumption: that the product will be reliable and safe. When this assumption is broken, no amount of features can compensate. Imagine a customer who loses their savings because of a product breach. That customer will not care about the next release cycle or the new user interface. They will care about trust, and once lost, it is nearly impossible to rebuild.

Embedding resilience in the product lifecycle also requires a mindset shift within teams. Product managers must act as advocates, ensuring that resilience does not get sacrificed in the race for faster releases. This can be challenging in environments where market competition is fierce and leadership demands rapid growth. Yet history shows that products built without resilience often grow fast and die faster. The dot-com era was filled with startups that dazzled with features but collapsed at the first major disruption. The lesson for today is clear: growth without resilience is unsustainable.

A key challenge lies in making resilience tangible for stakeholders who may not immediately see its value. Executives often focus on revenue growth, investors focus on market share, and engineers focus on delivery. The product manager must bridge these perspectives, articulating how resilience supports each. For executives, resilience protects brand reputation, which directly impacts revenue. For investors, resilience ensures continuity, making the product a safer bet for long-term returns. For engineers, resilience creates clarity, reducing the chaos of firefighting during crises. By framing resilience as a value multiplier rather than a cost, product managers can secure the buy-in necessary to embed it throughout the lifecycle.

Another dimension worth emphasizing is the evolving nature of threats. In the past, cyber risks were often limited to viruses or basic phishing schemes. Today, threats include sophisticated ransomware campaigns, supply chain attacks, insider threats, and state-sponsored espionage. The landscape changes so quickly that what was sufficient a year ago may already be outdated. This reality makes resilience even more crucial. A product cannot simply be secured once and left unattended. It must continuously adapt to new threats. Product managers must therefore build adaptability into the lifecycle itself, ensuring that resilience practices evolve alongside the product.

The Nigerian context again provides striking examples. Telecom companies handling millions of mobile money transactions have faced targeted attacks designed to exploit integration weaknesses. E-commerce platforms have been hit with denial-of-service attacks during high-traffic sales. Even government platforms have suffered disruptions from poor resilience planning. Each case illustrates the same truth: resilience cannot be an afterthought in digital economies where trust and continuity are paramount.

Yet resilience is not only defensive. Properly understood, it can be a source of differentiation. In markets crowded with similar features, the product that demonstrates consistent reliability, transparent incident handling, and proactive security measures will win trust. Customers increasingly make choices not just based on price or features but on confidence that their data and access are protected. Product managers who embrace resilience can thus position their products not only as useful but as trustworthy.

To achieve this, product managers must adopt a holistic view. Resilience is not achieved by technology alone. It involves people, processes, and culture. Teams must be trained, roles must be clear, and communication must be transparent. Processes such as regular drills, audits, and reviews must be embedded. Culturally, organizations must see resilience as everyone's responsibility, not just the IT departments. The product manager, as the integrator of perspectives, is uniquely placed to champion this holistic approach.

The journey toward cyber-resilient products is not without obstacles. Resource constraints, competing priorities, and resistance to change are common. But the alternative—products that collapse under attack is far worse. By framing resilience as a journey rather than a destination, product managers can build momentum. Small wins, such as implementing regular vulnerability testing or establishing clear incident communication protocols, can accumulate into a culture of resilience over time.

Ultimately, to understand cyber-resilience in the product lifecycle is to recognize that resilience is not a feature; it is a foundation. Just as houses are built with structural integrity in mind, products must be built with resilience as a core principle. Without it, the most beautiful design or innovative feature may crumble under pressure. With it, products can endure, adapt, and thrive in a world where threats are constant but opportunities remain vast.

1.1 The Cost of Ignoring Resilience

It is tempting for product teams to deprioritize resilience when resources are scarce or when pressure to ship is high. Many organizations convince themselves that resilience can wait until the product finds market traction. Yet history repeatedly shows that the cost of ignoring resilience far outweighs the cost of building it early.

Financial losses are often the most visible. A single data breach can result in millions of dollars in recovery costs, compensation, and lost revenue. For startups, these losses can be fatal. Investors withdraw, customers leave, and partnerships dissolve. For larger enterprises, the immediate cost may be survivable, but the long-term erosion of trust often proves more damaging.

Reputational damage can cripple even the most successful product. In a digital world where news spreads instantly, users are quick to abandon platforms that fail to protect them. Competitors capitalize on these failures, positioning themselves as safer alternatives. Rebuilding trust requires time, transparency, and significant investment—resources that many companies cannot afford to spare.

Regulatory consequences add another layer of risk. As governments strengthen data protection laws, non-compliance can attract hefty fines. The European Union's General Data Protection Regulation (GDPR) is perhaps the most well-known, but many African nations, including Nigeria with its Data Protection Act, are adopting stricter frameworks. A lack of resilience not only exposes products to attacks but also to penalties that can hinder growth.

For product managers, these costs highlight why resilience cannot be postponed. It is not a luxury reserved for mature companies but a necessity for survival. By making resilience a priority from day one, product managers save their organizations from the crippling effects of neglect.

1.2 Resilience as an Ongoing Commitment

Perhaps the most important truth about resilience is that it is never complete. Unlike a feature that can be developed, tested, and released, resilience is an ongoing commitment. Threats evolve, technologies change, and customer expectations shift. What made a product resilient last year may no longer be sufficient today.

This ongoing nature of resilience requires discipline. Teams must regularly revisit assumptions, update processes, and refine strategies. Continuous monitoring becomes essential, not only to detect incidents quickly but also to learn from near misses. Just as athletes train consistently to stay fit, products must be "trained" through regular testing, audits, and scenario planning to remain resilient.

It also requires humility. No team can anticipate every possible scenario. The willingness to learn from failures, both internal and external, is what distinguishes resilient organizations from fragile ones. When incidents occur, the question is not who to blame but how to adapt. Product managers must model this attitude, encouraging transparency and framing setbacks as opportunities to strengthen systems.

Finally, ongoing resilience depends on leadership. Organizations that view resilience as a checkbox exercise will always lag behind those that treat it as part of their culture. Leaders must consistently signal that resilience matters as much as growth. Product managers, in turn, must reinforce this message in their daily interactions during backlog prioritization, sprint reviews, and stakeholder presentations.

Resilience, then, is not a destination. It is a journey without a final stop. The most successful products will be those that treat resilience as a permanent companion, adjusting course as threats emerge, technologies evolve, and user trust becomes ever more precious.

Chapter 2

The Evolving Threat Landscape for Digital Products

To appreciate the urgency of cyber-resilience; product managers must first understand the nature of the threats facing modern products. The digital environment of today is not the same as it was five years ago. Threats evolve rapidly, shaped by new technologies, emerging economies, and the ingenuity of both attackers and defenders. For a product manager, this landscape is not an abstract backdrop; it is the terrain on which every decision, trade-off, and strategy must be executed.

In the early days of the internet, threats were often simple and unsophisticated. Viruses spread through floppy disks, basic phishing emails tricked the careless, and denial-of-service attacks were nuisances more than existential risks. Many businesses treated cybersecurity as a secondary concern, something to be handled by IT once the product had been launched and customers were onboard. That world no longer exists. Today, the scale and sophistication of threats have reached levels that can cripple entire industries overnight.

One of the most notable shifts has been the professionalization of cybercrime. No longer is the domain of isolated hackers operating from basements, cybercrime has become a global industry worth billions of dollars. Organized groups run operations with structures resembling legitimate businesses, complete with research divisions, customer support lines, and even money-back guarantees for criminal services. Ransomware-as-a-service, for example, allows attackers with limited technical expertise to rent powerful tools from more advanced operators. This means that the number of potential attackers has multiplied, and the barriers to entry have dropped significantly.

For product managers, this trend means that any product with data, users, or transactions is a potential target. It does not matter whether the product serves millions of customers or only a few hundred. If value exists, so does risk. Small startups often assume they are too insignificant to attract attention, but attackers frequently target smaller firms precisely because they expect weaker defenses.

Another major development is the rise of supply chain attacks. In a world where products depend on third-party libraries, cloud services, and APIs, attackers have discovered that compromising one link in the chain can provide access to thousands of products downstream. The SolarWinds breach of 2020 is a stark example, where attackers compromised a software vendor's update mechanism, infiltrating organizations around the world. For product managers, the lesson is sobering resilience is not only about what happens within your own team, but also about the trust you place in your partners and suppliers.

The threat landscape also reflects geopolitical tensions. State-sponsored actors increasingly target products that support critical infrastructure, communications, and financial systems. For product managers working in sensitive sectors like fintech, energy, or healthcare, this raises the stakes considerably. Attacks may not only aim to steal data but to disrupt economies or undermine trust in institutions. Nigeria's financial system, with its rapid adoption of digital platforms, has already seen attempts to exploit weak integration points between banks, fintech startups, and mobile money operators.

Social engineering remains another powerful weapon. Despite advances in technology, humans are often the weakest link in the chain. Phishing, spear-phishing, and business email compromise (BEC) attacks continue to succeed, not because systems are weak but because people can be manipulated. Product managers must recognize that resilience is not only technical. It involves building awareness among users, designing interfaces that help prevent mistakes, and ensuring that teams are trained to spot manipulation attempts.

Emerging technologies have created new opportunities but also new vulnerabilities. Artificial intelligence, for example, is a powerful tool for detecting anomalies and defending against attacks. Yet the same AI can be weaponized by attackers to automate phishing campaigns, create realistic fake identities, or even generate malicious code. Deepfakes, once a novelty, are now being used to impersonate executives and authorize fraudulent transactions. For a product manager, this means that resilience requires vigilance in both adopting new technologies and anticipating how they might be exploited.

The Internet of Things (IoT) represents another area of risk. Products that connect everyday objects; cars, refrigerators, security cameras expand the attack surface dramatically. Each device becomes a potential entry point into larger networks. The 2016 Mirai botnet, which harnessed thousands of insecure IoT devices to launch a massive, distributed denial-of-service (DDoS) attack, showed how vulnerable this ecosystem can be. As Nigerian companies adopt IoT for agriculture, logistics, and energy, product managers must understand that resilience extends to every connected sensor and device.

Cloud computing also reshapes the threat landscape. While cloud providers invest heavily in security, misconfigurations by product teams remain a leading cause of breaches. Open storage buckets, poorly secured APIs, and weak identity controls have exposed sensitive data repeatedly. The shift to remote work during the COVID-19 pandemic accelerated cloud adoption, but it also created opportunities for attackers to exploit gaps in configuration and oversight. For product managers, resilience in the cloud requires not only trust in providers but also disciplined processes within their own teams.

The evolving threat landscape places new responsibilities on product managers. It is no longer enough to be aware that "cybersecurity matters." A product manager must understand how specific threats intersect with their product's lifecycle.

During ideation, they must anticipate whether the product could become a target because of the type of data it collects or the services it enables. In design, they must push for architectures that minimize single points of failure. During development, they must advocate for secure coding practices and regular testing. At launch, they must ensure that monitoring and incident response are not left as afterthoughts. As the product grows, they must track new threats and adjust accordingly.

Crucially, product managers must also understand the human dimension of threats. Users will continue to fall for phishing emails if products do not guide them with clear warnings. Teams will continue to make configuration mistakes if training is absent. Executives will continue to underestimate risks if communication is filled with jargon. Product managers, by virtue of their cross-functional role, are in the best position to translate these risks into business language that resonates with decision-makers.

Another implication is the need for global awareness. Threats often originate beyond borders, and the digital nature of products means that Nigerian startups face the same risks as multinational corporations. A payment app in Lagos could be targeted by attackers in Eastern Europe, while a logistics platform in Abuja could be disrupted by a botnet originating in Asia. Product managers must therefore think globally, even if their customer base is primarily local.

The threat landscape will not stabilize; it will continue to evolve. Quantum computing, while still emerging, poses long-term risks to current encryption standards. Advances in machine learning will empower both defenders and attackers. Political instability in one region can trigger waves of cyberattacks that ripple globally. For product managers, the message is clear: resilience is not a one-time achievement but an ongoing discipline.

Those who ignore this reality risk being caught off guard. Those who embrace it position their products for longevity. The resilient product manager does not see threats as reasons for fear but as signals for preparation. By staying informed, building strong partnerships, and embedding resilience in every decision, product managers can navigate this shifting battlefield with confidence.

The story of the evolving threat landscape is ultimately one of constant adaptation. Attackers innovate, but so do defenders. The products that thrive will be those whose managers accept this reality, plan for it, and turn resilience into a defining feature of their value proposition.

2.1 The Economic and Social Impact of Cyber Threats

Cyber threats do not only affect individual companies; they reverberate across economies and societies. When a banking app suffers a data breach, customers may lose their savings, but the damage extends far beyond financial loss. Trust in digital financial systems weakens, adoption of innovative services slows, and regulators respond with stricter requirements that increase costs for every player in the ecosystem.

In Nigeria, this dynamic is particularly critical. The country's financial inclusion drive depends heavily on digital platforms, mobile money, online banking, and fintech innovations. A significant attack on one player can erode public trust in the entire sector, undoing years of progress. Similarly, attacks on e-commerce platforms not only harm merchants but also discourage consumers from embracing online shopping, limiting economic growth.

The social impact is equally profound. Cyberattacks on healthcare platforms can delay access to care, putting lives at risk. Breaches of educational systems can expose sensitive student information. Even disruptions to ride-hailing or delivery apps can affect livelihoods for thousands of workers who depend on digital platforms for income. Product managers must recognize that the products they build are not isolated tools but integral parts of social and economic systems. Their resilience, or lack of it, shapes more than just their companies—it shapes communities.

2.2 Why Awareness is Not Enough

It is one thing to be aware of the evolving threat landscape; it is another to act on that awareness consistently. Too often, organizations acknowledge risks but fail to allocate resources, time, or leadership attention to address them. Awareness without action is dangerous because it creates a false sense of security.

Product managers may attend conferences, read reports, or hear about breaches in the news. But unless this knowledge is translated into design decisions, testing protocols, and cross-functional collaboration, it does little to protect products. Resilience requires deliberate integration into strategy and execution. Awareness is only the first step.

The challenge lies in moving from abstract knowledge to concrete implementation. This means asking hard questions during roadmap discussions: Are resilience features being prioritized alongside new functionality? It means insisting on budgets for monitoring tools, training programs, and incident drills. It means being willing to delay a launch if resilience has not been adequately addressed.

For product managers, this shift requires courage. It is not always easy to argue for resilience when stakeholders push for speed and revenue. Yet leadership often involves saying what others overlook. By moving beyond awareness, product managers ensure that resilience becomes a lived practice rather than a theoretical ideal.

Chapter 3

Embedding Security into Product Strategy

Product strategy has often been described as the compass that guides a team through the chaotic journey of building, launching, and scaling products. It defines what problems to solve, who the product is for, and how to allocate resources to deliver value. Yet, in many organizations, security is treated as a separate track, something that runs parallel to strategy rather than being embedded within it. This disconnect is dangerous. Products that treat security as an add-on find themselves vulnerable not only to technical risks but also to strategic misalignment.

A product manager who fails to weave security into strategy may achieve short-term gains, faster releases, flashy features, early user adoption but the long-term consequences can be devastating. Customers may abandon the product at the first sign of insecurity. Regulators may impose restrictions that limit growth. Competitors may seize the opportunity to differentiate themselves as safer, more trustworthy alternatives. To prevent this, product managers must treat security as a foundational element of strategy, as inseparable from customer experience as usability or performance.

At the heart of embedding security into strategy is the recognition that security is not just about preventing attacks; it is about protecting the very value proposition of the product. Consider a fintech platform whose strategy is to build trust with underbanked populations. Every decision in its roadmap from onboarding processes to transaction flows must be evaluated against the risk of undermining that trust. A breach that exposes customer data does not only create technical debt; it erodes the credibility on which the entire strategy depends.

Embedding security also means reframing how trade-offs are considered. Product managers are constantly balancing competing priorities: speed versus quality, innovation versus stability, cost versus scalability. Too often, security is left out of this equation, treated as an invisible assumption rather than a visible priority. By making security explicit in strategic discussions, product managers force teams to confront the risks of neglect. For example, choosing a third-party API because it is cheaper may reduce short-term costs but increase long-term vulnerabilities. A strategy that embeds security would make such risks part of the decision framework.

In practice, embedding security into strategy begins with vision. If the product vision statement promises reliability, trust, or empowerment, then resilience and security must be integral to how that vision is pursued. Roadmaps should reflect not only feature development but also resilience milestones: security audits, compliance certifications, and recovery exercises. Metrics for success should include not just growth numbers but also measures of trust, uptime, and incident response readiness.

For product managers, this requires learning to speak multiple languages. To executives, security must be framed in terms of brand reputation, regulatory risk, and long-term profitability. To engineers, it must be articulated as clear requirements, technical debt reduction, and system integrity. To customers, it must be communicated as ease of use, transparency, and protection of their interests. Strategy becomes the unifying thread that ensures these perspectives are aligned toward a common goal.

The Nigerian tech ecosystem provides vivid lessons in the consequences of neglecting or embedding security. In 2022, a popular e-commerce platform faced backlash after customers reported fraudulent transactions linked to weak authentication flows. The company's strategy had focused heavily on expanding vendor networks and introducing discounts, but security was never positioned as a pillar of growth. The fallout was swift: customers abandoned the platform, vendors lost confidence, and regulators stepped in. By contrast, another Nigerian fintech startup made security part of its brand identity, proudly showcasing its compliance with the Nigeria Data Protection Act and adopting biometric verification for all users. This choice slowed onboarding slightly, but it created a reputation for safety that drew cautious customers and institutional investors.

A common mistake is to treat security as separate from business goals, as if resilience competes with growth. In reality, resilience strengthens growth by protecting the product's ability to deliver value over time. Aligning security with business objectives means asking: how does resilience support customer acquisition, retention, and monetization?

For instance, a healthcare product that stores patient records may embed security by adopting strict encryption standards. This not only prevents breaches but also becomes a selling point to hospitals and regulators. A logistics platform may invest in resilience by securing driver and route data, thereby assuring clients that operations will not be easily disrupted. In each case, resilience is positioned as an enabler, not a constraint.

Product managers must help stakeholders see this alignment. When leadership demands faster releases, the product manager must highlight the risk of reputational damage if those releases compromise security. When investors push for rapid scaling, the product manager must argue that scaling without resilience is like constructing a skyscraper on weak foundations. By embedding security into strategic narratives, product managers ensure that resilience is not sidelined but championed.

Embedding security in strategy is not only about documents and roadmaps. It is also about culture. A culture that values resilience treats every team member as a guardian of trust. Engineers write secure code not because they are told to, but because they see it as part of product quality. Designers prioritize clarity in user flows to prevent mistakes that attackers could exploit. Marketing teams avoid exaggerating claims that could backfire during a breach.

Creating this culture requires consistent reinforcement from product managers. Security milestones must be celebrated, not treated as invisible. Incident drills must be approached with seriousness, not as box-ticking exercises. Leaders must reward teams that raise security concerns early rather than punishing them for slowing progress. Over time, resilience becomes embedded not just in strategy but in organizational identity.

3.1 Two Strategic Dimensions Often Overlooked

1. The Role of Regulation as Strategic Leverage

Many organizations see regulation only as a burden. Yet, when framed strategically, compliance can become a competitive advantage. A Nigerian SaaS company that achieves ISO 27001 certification, for example, immediately positions itself as trustworthy to international clients. Embedding regulatory alignment into strategy not only avoids penalties but also opens doors to partnerships and markets that demand higher standards.

2. Anticipating the Future as Strategy, Not Prediction

Too often, product strategies are reactive, responding only to present needs. But resilience requires looking ahead. Product managers must anticipate how emerging technologies such as artificial intelligence, quantum computing, or blockchain might reshape threats and opportunities. Embedding security into strategy means building adaptability, ensuring the product can pivot as threats evolve. This forward-looking approach is not about predicting the future perfectly but about preparing for uncertainty.

3.2 Case Study 1: Fintech Growth Without Resilience

In 2021, a West African fintech startup achieved rapid success by offering instant loans through a mobile app. Its strategy focused on speed of disbursement and ease of onboarding. The growth numbers were impressive, and the company attracted investors quickly. Yet, resilience was missing from its strategy. Customer data was stored with weak encryption, and there were no formal incident response plans. Within a year, attackers exploited these weaknesses, stealing customer records and publishing them online. The breach triggered regulatory scrutiny, lawsuits, and massive reputational damage. Investors withdrew, and the company never recovered.

For product managers, this case underscores the danger of separating growth strategy from security strategy. What looked like market leadership was actually built on fragile foundations. Had resilience been embedded from day one, the company might have sustained its growth trajectory instead of collapsing under its own vulnerabilities.

3.3 Case Study 2: A Nigerian HealthTech Platform's Strategic Win

By contrast, a Nigerian healthtech startup building electronic medical record systems chose to embed security into its strategy from inception. Recognizing the sensitivity of patient data, the team adopted international encryption standards, implemented multi-factor authentication, and invested in regular third-party audits. These decisions slowed their release schedule and increased short-term costs, but they yielded long-term advantages. Hospitals and clinics, often skeptical of digital solutions, were reassured by the company's transparency and compliance posture. As a result, the startup secured government partnerships and became one of the first Nigerian firms to export its healthtech solutions regionally.

Here, resilience was not just protection; it was leverage. By embedding security into strategy, the company positioned itself as credible, trustworthy, and future-ready. Product managers in other sectors can draw a clear lesson: resilience is not an expense to be minimized but an asset to be maximized.

3.4 Case Study 3: Global Example — The Apple Approach

Globally, Apple has demonstrated how embedding security into product strategy can become a brand differentiator. Features such as on-device encryption, secure enclave chips, and transparent privacy policies are not treated as technical footnotes but as strategic pillars. Customers now associate Apple products with privacy and security, a perception that directly influences purchasing decisions. Even when competitors offer cheaper devices with more features, many users choose Apple because they believe their data will be safer.

This example illustrates how security embedded into strategy can transform into a competitive moat. For product managers, the takeaway is clear: resilience is not only about preventing loss but about generating value through trust.

3.5 Case Study 4: A Nigerian E-Commerce Platform's Turning Point

An e-commerce platform in Nigeria learned resilience the hard way. Initially, its product strategy was centered on vendor acquisition and aggressive discounts. Security was considered later. After several cases of fraudulent vendor accounts and customer payment disputes, the platform faced backlash. Sales declined, and regulators began asking questions. In response, the company pivoted strategically: it introduced stricter vendor verification, partnered with payment processors to enforce stronger authentication, and ran a public campaign about its new "trusted marketplace" initiative.

Although costly, this pivot eventually restored customer confidence and stabilized the business. For product managers, this example shows that embedding resilience late is possible, but the costs are significantly higher. It is always better to build with resilience in mind rather than retrofit it after a crisis.

Chapter 4

Secure Design Principles for Product Managers

Design is often celebrated as the art of making products usable, intuitive, and delightful. For product managers, design has traditionally meant ensuring that customer journeys are smooth, that features are accessible, and that interfaces make sense even to first-time users. Yet, in today's digital ecosystem, design must go beyond aesthetics and usability. It must also embody resilience. A well-designed product is not only one that people can use easily but one that people can trust. Secure design principles, therefore, are not technical extras but central to the product manager's mandate.

The idea of secure design is rooted in prevention. It is far easier and more cost-effective to build resilience into the design phase than to attempt to patch vulnerabilities after release. Studies consistently show that fixing security issues in production is exponentially more expensive than addressing them in design. More importantly, design decisions shape user behavior. A poorly designed authentication flow, for example, may encourage users to choose weak passwords or reuse them across platforms, creating vulnerabilities that attackers can exploit. Conversely, a thoughtfully designed flow can nudge users toward safer practices without causing friction.

For product managers, secure design begins with mindset. It requires thinking about how malicious actors might misuse or exploit the product, not just how customers will use it. This perspective, often called "designing for abuse cases," encourages teams to anticipate not only intended behaviors but also unintended ones. If a ride-hailing app allows easy account creation, how might fraudsters exploit that to create fake accounts? If a healthcare platform allows doctors to upload records, how might attackers manipulate that feature by inserting false data? By asking these questions early, product managers ensure that resilience is not an afterthought.

One of the foundational principles of secure design is **least privilege**. This principle dictates that users and systems should only have the minimum access necessary to perform their tasks. While it may be tempting to grant broad permissions in the name of convenience, doing so creates unnecessary risks. A Nigerian fintech that once allowed customer service staff full access to transaction histories learned this the hard way when an insider leaked sensitive information. After the incident, the company revised its design to enforce least privilege, limiting staff access to only the data required for resolving disputes.

Another principle is **secure defaults**. When given options, most users will stick with default settings. If those defaults are insecure, the majority of users will unknowingly be exposed. For instance, if two-factor authentication (2FA) is offered but not enabled by default, adoption rates remain low. A more resilient design would make 2FA the default while still allowing opt-out for advanced users. Product managers must advocate for secure defaults even when they add slight friction, because defaults shape the baseline security posture of the product.

Privacy by design is equally critical. Regulations such as the EU's GDPR and Nigeria's Data Protection Act mandate that privacy be embedded into design rather than bolted on later. For product managers, this means ensuring that only the data necessary for functionality is collected, that users are informed about how their data will be used, and that retention policies are clear. An educational app that collects student data, for example, must avoid storing unnecessary personal identifiers. By designing data minimization, the product reduces the impact of potential breaches.

Usability and security must not be seen as opposites. Poorly designed security features can backfire by driving users toward unsafe workarounds. If password requirements are excessively complex, users may resort to writing them down or reusing them across platforms. A resilient design balances protection with convenience, creating flows that guide users naturally toward safer practices. Biometrics, for instance, have become popular because they offer both security and ease of use. Product managers must champion solutions that protect without alienating customers.

Consider the Nigerian banking sector, where apps compete fiercely for user adoption. Some banks initially required long, cumbersome processes for online transfers in the name of security. Customers complained, adoption lagged, and competitors offering smoother experiences gained market share. Eventually, the banks redesigned their flows to combine strong authentication with streamlined user journeys, showing that security and usability can reinforce rather than contradict each other.

Secure design also extends to architecture. Decisions about whether to centralize or decentralize data, how to structure APIs, and what kind of logging systems to implement all have security implications. Product managers may not write the code, but they must understand the strategic impact of these choices. Centralized systems may be easier to manage but create single points of failure. Decentralized systems may offer resilience but increase complexity. A product manager's role is to ensure that these trade-offs are discussed openly and aligned with the overall product vision.

Technology alone cannot guarantee resilience; human behavior is always part of the equation. Secure design requires anticipating how real people—customers, employees, and even attackers—will interact with the system. For example, social engineering remains one of the most common attack vectors. A product that relies solely on technical safeguards without educating users about phishing will remain vulnerable.

Product managers must therefore integrate human factors into design. This may involve clear warning messages, intuitive interfaces for reporting suspicious activity, or built-in nudges that discourage risky behavior. A global messaging platform that displays warnings when users attempt to click on suspicious links demonstrates this principle well. In Nigeria, telecom providers have implemented similar warnings for fraudulent SMS messages, showing how secure design can be localized to address specific threats.

Design does not end when a product is launched. Continuous validation is essential to ensure that design choices remain effective as threats evolve. Regular usability testing should include not only user experience goals but also security considerations. Penetration testing, red teaming, and bug bounty programs provide valuable feedback loops that reveal weaknesses in design. For product managers, this means treating resilience as an ongoing design criterion rather than a one-time checklist.

4.1 Two Areas Often Overlooked in Secure Design

1. The Hidden Risks of Integrations

Many products today are built on integrations with third-party services—payment processors, analytics tools, cloud storage. While these integrations accelerate development, they also create hidden risks. If a third-party service is compromised, the product may be indirectly affected. Product managers must insist on due diligence when choosing partners, ensuring that integrations do not become backdoors into the system.

2. Accessibility and Inclusive Security

Secure design must also account for diverse user groups. An authentication flow that assumes high digital literacy may alienate older users or those with limited exposure to technology. In Nigeria, where literacy and connectivity levels vary widely, product managers must ensure that security features are accessible to all. This could mean offering multiple authentication methods, biometrics, PINs, or SMS codes so that resilience does not exclude vulnerable groups.

4.2 Designing for Failure and Recovery

One of the realities of secure design is that no matter how well a system is built, failures will occur. Servers may crash, authentication tokens may expire, or unexpected bugs may expose vulnerabilities. What distinguishes resilient products from fragile ones is not the absence of failure but the ability to recover gracefully.

Designing for failure requires imagining worst-case scenarios during the design phase. What happens if a user is locked out of their account? What if a database temporarily goes offline? What if a malicious actor tries to overwhelm the system with requests? By modeling these situations, teams can design safeguards that prevent small issues from escalating into crises.

A resilient authentication flow, for example, provides fallback options such as recovery codes, alternative verification methods, or secure customer support channels. A resilient payment system ensures that failed transactions are rolled back automatically, avoiding duplicate charges or data inconsistencies. For product managers, the challenge is to make recovery invisible to the customer wherever possible, so that users continue to trust the product even during disruption.

Another area often overlooked is the role of transparency in secure design. Customers do not expect perfection, but they do expect honesty. When products are designed with transparency in mind, users are more likely to trust them, even in the face of incidents. Transparency begins with clear communication: privacy settings should be easy to understand, error messages should explain what went wrong without exposing sensitive details, and updates about incidents should be timely and respectful.

A Nigerian fintech platform once suffered a temporary outage that left customers unable to withdraw funds for several hours. Instead of staying silent, the company issued a clear, concise update explaining the issue and outlining steps being taken to resolve it. Customers were frustrated, but many appreciated the honesty and continued to use the service. Contrast this with a global social media company that concealed breaches for months; when the truth eventually emerged, the reputational damage far outweighed the technical issue itself.

For product managers, embedding transparency means working with designers and communicators to ensure that trust is built into every interaction. Customers should feel that the product respects them, not manipulates them. Transparency, in this sense, is not weakness but strength, it demonstrates confidence, accountability, and respect for the people the product serves.

Chapter 5

Building Resilient Architectures and Infrastructures

Architecture is the skeleton of every product, the structure upon which features, user flows, and business value are built. If the skeleton is fragile, no matter how elegant the design or how innovative the features are, the product cannot withstand shocks. Infrastructure, in turn, provides the foundation upon which architecture rests, the servers, cloud services, networks, and data centers that bring a product to life. Together, architecture and infrastructure determine whether a product can deliver value consistently, scale sustainably, and recover quickly when things go wrong.

For years, product managers were rarely expected to understand architectural or infrastructural decisions. These matters were delegated to engineering teams, while PMs focused on features, markets, and customer experience. But as resilience has become a defining factor in product success, product managers cannot remain distant from these conversations. While they may not dictate technical specifications, they must influence the principles guiding them, ensuring that resilience is never sacrificed for short-term gains.

At the heart of resilient architecture is the principle of **redundancy**. Redundancy ensures that when one component fails, another can take its place without interrupting service. This can apply at multiple levels: redundant servers, redundant data storage, redundant network paths. To a customer, redundancy is invisible, but it is often the reason they continue to trust a product during an outage. A Nigerian telecom provider once demonstrated this when a fiber cut disrupted internet service from one region. Because the company had invested in redundant routes, customers experienced only minor delays rather than a total blackout.

Closely related is **fault tolerance**, the ability of a system to continue operating even when parts of it fail. A payment processor, for instance, may lose one node in its cluster, but transactions are rerouted to functioning nodes without customers noticing. Fault tolerance requires thoughtful design, often involving distributed systems, automated failover mechanisms, and robust monitoring. For product managers, the implication is clear: resilience must be prioritized in architectural decisions, even if it increases initial costs or development complexity.

Scalability is another cornerstone of resilient architecture. A product that works flawlessly with 10,000 users but collapses with 100,000 is not truly resilient. Scalability requires anticipating growth and designing systems that can expand without degradation in performance or security. Cloud infrastructure has made scalability more achievable, with elastic services that adjust capacity dynamically. Yet, scalability must be planned, not assumed. Product managers must ensure that growth projections are factored into architectural discussions and that resilience is considered not just in present operations but in future scenarios.

Security is intertwined with architecture. Decisions about how to partition systems, where to place firewalls, and how to encrypt data all affect resilience. Poorly segmented architectures allow attackers who breach one system to move laterally across the network. Strong segmentation, on the other hand, contains breaches and limits damage. Similarly, encrypting data at rest and in transit ensures that even if attackers gain access, the data remains unusable. Product managers must therefore ask critical questions: How is data stored? How is it transmitted? What barriers prevent attackers from moving freely within our systems?

Monitoring and observability play a crucial role. A resilient architecture is not only about preventing failures but also about detecting them quickly. Logs, metrics, and alerts provide visibility into the health of the system. Without visibility, failures may linger undetected until they escalate into crises. For example, an e-commerce company in Nigeria discovered a vulnerability only after fraudulent transactions spiked, by which time the damage was severe. Had robust monitoring been in place, anomalies could have been detected earlier, minimizing loss. For product managers, observability should be treated as a core feature of the product's infrastructure, not an optional enhancement.

Resilient infrastructures also embrace the concept of **DevSecOps**, integrating security into development and operations workflows. This approach ensures that resilience is not bolted on at the end but embedded throughout the lifecycle. Automated testing, continuous integration, and deployment pipelines that include security checks make resilience part of daily operations. For product managers, supporting a DevSecOps culture means advocating for investments in tooling, training, and processes that reinforce resilience at every stage.

The cloud has revolutionized resilience but introduced new risks. While cloud providers offer robust infrastructure, misconfigurations by teams remain a leading cause of breaches. Open storage buckets, excessive permissions, and weak access controls are frequent culprits. Product managers must therefore balance the opportunities of the cloud; elasticity, redundancy, scalability with the discipline required to configure and manage it securely. Asking the right questions about cloud strategy, insisting on audits, and planning for multi-cloud or hybrid deployments can make the difference between resilience and fragility.

Local context also matters. In Nigeria, frequent power outages and unreliable connectivity mean that infrastructure decisions cannot simply mirror those made in Silicon Valley. Resilient infrastructures must plan for these realities, whether through backup power solutions, localized data centers, or offline functionality in apps. A fintech startup that designed its app to work even with intermittent connectivity gained a competitive edge, not because it had the most advanced features but because it respected the infrastructural realities of its users.

Too often, architectural discussions focus solely on preventing failures. While prevention is critical, no system is immune to disruption. Recovery must therefore be a central design principle. Recovery involves more than restarting systems; it includes restoring data, verifying integrity, and communicating with users. Backup strategies are essential, but backups are only useful if they can be restored quickly and reliably. A bank that takes days to restore systems after an outage risk losing not only customers but also regulatory approval.

For product managers, this means asking pointed questions: How often are backups tested? What is our recovery time objective (RTO)? What is our recovery point objective (RPO)? These terms may seem technical, but they translate directly into user experience. An RTO of 24 hours means customers may be without service for a full day. An RPO of 12 hours means data entered within that window could be lost. By understanding and influencing these parameters, product managers ensure that resilience aligns with customer expectations.

Building resilient architectures and infrastructures is not cheap. Redundancy, fault tolerance, monitoring, and backups all require investment. Yet the cost of resilience must be weighed against the cost of failure. A single breach or outage can cost far more than years of preventive investment. Product managers must therefore frame resilience not as a sunk cost but as insurance and value creation. Resilient products attract cautious customers, reassure investors, and open doors to regulated markets. The return on investment is not always immediate, but it is real.

5.1 Why Teams, Processes, and Decision-Making Are as Important as Technology

When people talk about architecture and infrastructure, they often default to thinking about servers, cloud providers, or software frameworks. Yet technology is only one dimension of resilience. The human element, teams, processes, and decision-making structures often determines whether an architecture is truly resilient or dangerously fragile. A beautifully designed system can still collapse if the team managing it lacks the discipline to enforce security controls, monitor anomalies, or respond to alerts in time.

In many organizations, product managers assume that once an architecture is set up by engineers, it will automatically deliver resilience. But architecture is a living entity. Configurations change, integrations are added, updates roll out, and new dependencies emerge. Each of these requires human oversight. For example, one Nigerian financial institution suffered an outage not because its cloud infrastructure failed but because an administrator accidentally disabled a critical configuration without a rollback process. The architecture itself was sound, but the lack of process discipline and human safeguards undermined its resilience.

Product managers must therefore treat teams and processes as integral to resilience. They should ensure that architectural decisions are documented that configuration changes follow formal approval workflows, and that responsibilities for monitoring and response are clearly assigned. Cross-functional drills involving engineering, operations, and customer support teams help align people with the architecture's intended resilience. Without such human readiness, even the strongest infrastructure becomes brittle.

Moreover, decision-making culture plays a role. In some organizations, engineers hesitate to raise concerns about resilience because leadership prioritizes speed. In others, security warnings are dismissed as alarmist until a breach occurs. Product managers, by virtue of their role, must create a culture where resilience is valued as much as innovation. This requires consistently advocating for resilience in strategy meetings, framing it not as a technical issue but as a customer trust imperative. When leadership understands that resilience protects revenue and reputation, decision-making begins to support rather than undermine architecture.

Ultimately, resilient architecture is not just about what technology is deployed but about how humans interact with it. The best infrastructures fail when people fail to manage them responsibly. The most ordinary infrastructures survive crises when people are disciplined, alert, and aligned with resilience goals. For product managers, acknowledging the human element is essential if architectural resilience is to be more than a blueprint on paper.

5.2 Embedding Resilience in the Broader Ecosystem of Regulations, Customers, and Market Expectations

While resilience is often framed in technical terms, redundancy, fault tolerance, monitoring, the reality is that products do not exist in isolation. They operate within a larger ecosystem that includes regulators, customers, competitors, and broader market expectations. If architectures are built without considering these external forces, they may be technically strong but strategically fragile.

Regulations increasingly shape how infrastructures are designed and maintained. In Nigeria, the Data Protection Act sets requirements for how personal data must be stored and secured. Globally, frameworks like ISO 27001 and NIST standards influence what "good" architecture looks like. A resilient infrastructure, therefore, is not just one that works well but one that complies with evolving regulatory expectations. Product managers must anticipate these regulations and advocate for architectures that can meet them without costly overhauls. For instance, building systems with flexible data governance controls from the start allows products to adapt quickly when new regulations emerge.

Customers are another critical part of the ecosystem. Users today are more informed about security and resilience than ever before. They ask whether their data is encrypted, whether platforms provide multi-factor authentication, and whether service disruptions are handled transparently. A resilient architecture must be designed not only to withstand threats but also to meet customer expectations of safety and reliability. If a competitor offers visibly stronger resilience features, customers may abandon products that appear weaker, regardless of whether those weaknesses are ever exploited.

Market expectations also evolve rapidly. For example, cloud-native architectures are becoming a baseline expectation in many industries. Products that continue relying on outdated monolithic infrastructures risk being seen as unreliable, even if they still function adequately. Similarly, as hybrid and multi-cloud deployments become more common, resilience strategies that fail to embrace these shifts may appear outdated. Product managers must therefore view architecture not only through the lens of technology but also through the lens of perception. The most resilient infrastructure is one that delivers technical stability while simultaneously meeting regulatory requirements, satisfying customer demands, and aligning with market trends.

In short, resilience cannot be reduced to a technical checklist. It is a socio-technical reality that requires engaging with laws, people, and competitive landscapes. Product managers who understand this broader context will not only safeguard their products from disruption but also position them as leaders in markets where trust and compliance increasingly define success.

Chapter 6

Governance, Risk, and Compliance (GRC) in Product Development

Governance, risk, and compliance, commonly known as GRC are often spoken of in boardrooms and policy documents, but they may feel distant from the day-to-day realities of product management. Yet, for a product to be truly cyber-resilient, GRC is not a distant concern. It is the framework that connects organizational values, regulatory expectations, and operational discipline into a coherent strategy. For product managers, engaging in GRC is not optional; it is an essential part of ensuring that products are trusted, lawful, and sustainable.

Governance defines how decisions are made, who has authority, and what processes guide the product's lifecycle. It ensures that resilience is not dependent on the instincts of individuals but is embedded in structures that outlast them. In practical terms, governance means clear policies about who can approve architectural changes, how incident responses are escalated, and what criteria must be met before launching new features. Without governance, resilience becomes inconsistent, strong when the right person is involved, weak when they are absent.

Risk management, the second pillar, involves identifying, assessing, and mitigating potential threats. While many product managers think of risk only in financial terms, digital products risk spans data breaches, downtime, reputational harm, and regulatory penalties. Effective risk management requires anticipating what could go wrong, measuring the likelihood and impact, and designing controls to reduce exposure. For example, a Nigerian fintech company processing online payments must assess not only the risk of transaction fraud but also the risk of downtime during high-volume events like Black Friday sales. Both risks have direct implications for customer trust and business continuity.

Compliance is the third pillar. It involves meeting the legal, regulatory, and contractual requirements that govern product operations. In an interconnected digital economy, compliance is not just about avoiding fines; it is about signaling credibility. Customers, investors, and partners look to compliance as evidence that an organization takes security and resilience seriously. A healthtech platform, for instance, that can demonstrate compliance with Nigeria's Data Protection Act and international frameworks like HIPAA or GDPR is more likely to gain the trust of hospitals and patients.

The challenge for product managers is that GRC can seem abstract, filled with acronyms, checklists, and legal language. But behind the complexity lies a simple truth: GRC protects the product from chaos. Governance ensures decisions are accountable. Risk management ensures threats are anticipated. Compliance ensures operations are lawful and credible. Together, they form the backbone of resilience.

In practice, product managers must learn to work with GRC stakeholders; compliance officers, legal teams, risk analysts and integrate their expertise into product decisions. This does not mean PMs need to become lawyers or auditors, but they must know enough to ask the right questions. If a new feature involves collecting biometric data, what regulations apply? If a third-party integration introduces potential vulnerabilities, what risks are being accepted? If a cloud vendor cannot guarantee up time, what contractual protections exist? By asking these questions, PMs bring GRC into the product conversation rather than leaving it as a separate track.

One tension that often arises is between GRC and agile methodologies. Agile emphasizes speed, iteration, and adaptability. GRC emphasizes structure, documentation, and accountability. At first glance, these priorities appear incompatible. Product managers working in fast-moving startups may resist GRC, fearing it will slow innovation. Yet, true resilience requires balancing agility with accountability.

Bridging GRC with agile practices means integrating governance, risk, and compliance into sprints rather than treating them as separate gates at the end. Risk assessments can be included in backlog prioritization. Compliance requirements can be translated into acceptance criteria for user stories. Governance policies can define when "done" truly means done. By embedding GRC into agile workflows, PMs ensure that resilience is maintained without sacrificing speed.

Several Nigerian fintech startups have successfully adopted this approach. Instead of waiting until regulators knock on the door, they bring compliance officers into sprint planning. Instead of treating risk reviews as annual events, they hold lightweight risk discussions at each release milestone. This integration prevents last-minute crises and reduces the perception of GRC as a blocker. Instead, it becomes part of the rhythm of product development.

Product managers must also navigate the intersection of global standards and local realities. International frameworks like ISO 27001, NIST Cybersecurity Framework, and GDPR provide valuable benchmarks. They offer common languages for resilience and make products more credible in global markets. Yet, local contexts such as Nigeria's Data Protection Act or sector-specific guidelines from the Central Bank of Nigeria—cannot be ignored.

The challenge lies in aligning both. A Nigerian SaaS company targeting global clients must meet ISO standards while also ensuring compliance with Nigerian law. A healthtech product working across West Africa must navigate different regulatory landscapes in each country. For PMs, this requires strategic thinking: which standards provide the broadest coverage? Which local laws create unique requirements? By making these considerations part of the product strategy, PMs prevent costly redesigns or market restrictions later.

One area often overlooked in GRC discussions is the hidden value of governance as a trust-building mechanism. Customers and partners rarely ask for detailed technical diagrams of architectures, but they do want assurance that someone is accountable if things go wrong. Strong governance provides that assurance.

For example, when a Nigerian bank rolled out a new mobile app, it made public its governance structure for digital services: a dedicated oversight committee, escalation protocols, and named executives responsible for resilience. Customers may not have understood every detail, but the transparency created confidence. Governance here was not just an internal tool but an external signal of accountability.

Product managers can leverage governance in a similar way. By communicating governance structures who handle incidents, how decisions are made, what accountability frameworks exist; they reassure stakeholders that resilience is not left to chance. Governance thus becomes a competitive differentiator, showing that the product is not only innovative but responsibly managed.

6.1 Compliance Beyond Avoiding Penalties: How Regulatory Alignment Strengthens Innovation and Market Access

When most product teams think of compliance, the first reaction is fear; fear of penalties, audits, or regulatory shutdowns. Compliance becomes a box to tick in order to avoid punishment. But this narrow perspective misses a powerful truth: compliance, when embraced strategically, can unlock innovation and market opportunities.

Consider the case of a Nigerian healthtech company that sought to partner with international NGOs on digital health programs. The NGOs required proof of compliance with global data privacy standards. Because the company had invested early in aligning its infrastructure with both Nigeria's Data Protection Act and GDPR principles, it was able to demonstrate readiness. The result was not just avoidance of penalties but access to new markets, new funding, and international credibility.

Compliance can also spark innovation. When the Central Bank of Nigeria introduced new guidelines for digital financial transactions, some startups saw them as hurdles. Others, however, used the opportunity to innovate in authentication flows, building features that were not only compliant but also improved user trust. These startups gained market share because they aligned with regulations faster and more creatively than their competitors.

For product managers, the lesson is clear: compliance is not a dead weight on innovation. It is a framework that shapes responsible creativity. By anticipating compliance requirements, PMs can design products that meet current laws and adapt quickly to future ones. Instead of resisting compliance, they can turn it into a competitive advantage.

6.2 Integrating GRC into Organizational Culture: From Policy Documents to Everyday Practice

Another area often overlooked is the cultural dimension of GRC. Too often, governance, risk, and compliance live in policy binders, training slides, or annual audit reports, far removed from everyday product work. But unless GRC is embedded into daily practice, it cannot deliver true resilience.

Culture begins with leadership. If executives treat GRC as a burden, teams will see it as a distraction. If leaders model accountability, encourage risk awareness, and celebrate compliance milestones, teams will internalize these values.

Product managers play a central role here, translating GRC principles into daily rituals. A backlog grooming session that includes risk discussion, a sprint review that checks compliance criteria, or a design workshop that considers governance implications, these are cultural signals that resilience is part of "how we work," not an afterthought.

Practical examples highlight this. A Nigerian fintech implemented a culture of "risk champions" within each squad. These champions were not compliance officers but regular team members trained to raise risk questions during daily standups. This lightweight integration turned risk management into a shared responsibility rather than a siloed function. Over time, the company built a culture where risk awareness was as natural as checking for bugs.

Organizational culture also determines how failures are handled. In firms where mistakes are punished harshly, teams hide incidents until they spiral out of control. In firms where mistakes are treated as learning opportunities, incidents are reported quickly, contained early, and used to strengthen systems. Embedding GRC into culture means building trust; trust that teams can raise concerns without fear, trust that accountability is clear, and trust that resilience is valued as much as innovation.

Chapter 7

Incident Management and Product Continuity Planning

Even the most secure and well-designed products will, at some point, face disruptions. These may come in the form of cyberattacks, outages, misconfigurations, insider threats, or unexpected external shocks like infrastructure failures. The question is not whether incidents will happen but how effectively a product team can respond when they do. For product managers, incident management and continuity planning are the twin pillars of resilience. They ensure that, when crises strike, customers experience disruption as minimal, communication as clear, and recovery as swift.

An incident is any unplanned event that disrupts normal operations or threatens the confidentiality, integrity, or availability of systems. While some incidents are minor, others can escalate into full-blown crises with financial, reputational, and legal consequences. In the digital economy, a single incident can undo years of brand building. Customers expect products to falter occasionally, but they do not forgive silence, confusion, or incompetence in response.

Incident management begins long before an incident occurs. Preparation is the foundation. Teams must have clear playbooks that define what counts as an incident, how incidents are classified, and what steps should be taken for each level of severity. Without preparation, responses become ad hoc, leading to delays, duplication of effort, and costly mistakes. A Nigerian bank once suffered a system outage that lasted several hours. Because the incident response plan was outdated and poorly communicated, different teams worked at cross-purposes, worsening customer frustration. Contrast this with another bank that rehearses response drills quarterly; when an outage occurred, the team restored services in under an hour with transparent updates to customers.

Communication is one of the most overlooked aspects of incident management. Technical teams may focus on fixing the problem, but if customers are left in the dark, trust erodes rapidly. Product managers must therefore play a central role in communication, crafting messages that are accurate, timely, and empathetic. The goal is to reassure customers that the issue is being handled, explain the impact clearly, and provide realistic timelines for resolution. Silence or vague assurances often fuel speculation and distrust, compounding the damage.

Continuity planning extends beyond managing incidents to ensuring the product can operate even during disruption. Business continuity asks: how do we keep critical functions running when systems are compromised? For example, a payments platform may route transactions through backup servers if the primary system fails. A logistics app may allow offline order recording during network outages, syncing data once connectivity resumes. Continuity planning requires identifying the most critical services and building redundancies to protect them.

Product managers must champion continuity by asking practical questions: Which features are mission-critical for customers? How quickly must these features be restored in case of failure? What alternatives exist if full functionality cannot be maintained? Continuity is not about eliminating disruption but about minimizing its impact so customers retain confidence in the product.

Another key element is learning from incidents. Too many organizations treat incidents as isolated events, rushing to restore operations but failing to analyze root causes. True resilience requires structured post-mortems that identify what went wrong, why it went wrong, and how similar issues can be prevented. Importantly, post-mortems must be blameless. The goal is not to punish individuals but to improve systems. Product managers must lead this cultural shift, ensuring that every incident becomes an opportunity to strengthen resilience rather than a source of fear.

The Nigerian context provides numerous examples of the importance of continuity. In sectors where infrastructure is unreliable, products that anticipate disruptions thrive. An agricultural fintech built for farmers in rural areas designed its app to function offline, allowing farmers to record transactions without internet access. This foresight turned continuity into a competitive advantage, as competitors struggled in regions with poor connectivity. Similarly, during power outages in Lagos, fintech companies that had invested in generator-backed data centers and cloud redundancy were able to maintain service while others faltered.

Globally, some of the most admired companies are those that have turned incident response into an art. Amazon Web Services (AWS), despite occasional outages, maintains credibility by issuing detailed post-incident reports that explain what happened, what was fixed, and how recurrence will be prevented. This transparency builds confidence, even when failures occur. For product managers, the lesson is that incidents need not destroy trust if they are handled with professionalism and openness.

One of the most critical, yet often neglected, aspects of incident management is the creation of playbooks and escalation structures. In moments of crisis, time is the most valuable asset. Teams that must pause to debate responsibilities, approval chains, or next steps waste precious minutes that can determine the severity of the incident's impact.

Playbooks provide predefined steps for common scenarios such as a ransomware attack, a denial-of-service event, or a payment processor failure. They detail who should be alerted, what immediate actions must be taken, and how communication flows to internal and external stakeholders. Escalation structures define when an incident moves from frontline responders to executive leadership or external partners. By rehearsing these playbooks through drills, teams reduce uncertainty and improve coordination.

Product managers may not draft the technical details, but they must ensure playbooks exist, are updated, and align with customer promises. For example, if a company promises 99.9 percent uptime, playbooks must reflect the urgency required to meet that target. Escalation chains must also be realistic. If executives are unreachable during crises, decision-making stalls. PMs must advocate for structures where authority is distributed appropriately to allow rapid response.

Continuity is too often treated as an optional feature, a nice-to-have for enterprises but unnecessary for startups. This mindset is dangerous. In reality, continuity is a core part of customer value. Customers may not explicitly ask for backup systems, offline functionality, or redundant servers, but they assume the product will work when they need it most. When this assumption is broken, loyalty evaporates.

Product managers must therefore embed continuity into product strategy, not as a hidden technical detail but as a visible part of the value proposition. A fintech app that advertises "always available transactions" or a logistics platform that guarantees "no lost orders even when offline" differentiates itself by making continuity explicit. By framing continuity as part of customer experience, PMs shift it from a hidden cost to a competitive advantage.

Continuity planning also involves partnerships. No product operates in isolation. Payment apps rely on banks, logistics platforms rely on transport networks, and healthtech tools rely on clinics. Continuity requires assessing these dependencies and building agreements that ensure resilience across the ecosystem. Service-level agreements (SLAs), vendor audits, and backup partnerships become critical tools in continuity planning.

By embedding continuity into strategy, product managers not only reduce risk but also elevate trust as a core differentiator. In competitive markets, the product that customers believe will "always be there" wins loyalty even against faster or cheaper rivals.

7.1 The Role of Customers in Incident Response and Continuity: Educating, Informing, and Empowering Users During Crises

When organizations think of incident management, the focus often narrows to internal teams, engineers, compliance officers, executives. Customers are seen merely as recipients of updates. Yet, in reality, customers play a central role in resilience. They are not passive observers; they are active participants whose behavior during an incident can either minimize or magnify the impact.

A customer who understands how to reset credentials quickly is less likely to panic if their account is compromised. A merchant who knows how to use an offline mode will continue transacting during a connectivity outage. Conversely, uninformed customers may flood support lines, spread misinformation on social media, or abandon the product altogether.

Educating customers before incidents occur is therefore a form of resilience. Product managers must work with marketing and customer support to design simple guides, FAQs, and in-app prompts that prepare users for disruptions. For example, a fintech app can provide clear instructions on how to use backup payment channels if the primary system goes down. A healthtech platform can publish simple checklists for patients on how to retrieve records in case of temporary unavailability.

During incidents, transparency is vital. Customers need updates that are honest, specific, and reassuring. Telling users "we are aware of issues" without context often fuels frustration. Instead, communication should explain the nature of the issue in terms customers understand, provide timelines for resolution, and offer alternatives if available. Nigerian telecom companies, for example, have improved customer trust by sending SMS updates during outages, explaining the problem and expected recovery time.

Finally, empowering customers means involving them in the feedback loop after incidents. Post-incident surveys, customer forums, and public debriefs allow organizations to learn how disruptions were experienced and how resilience can be improved. This not only strengthens systems but also deepens trust by showing customers that their voices shape recovery strategies. Product managers who treat customers as partners in resilience build products that are not only technically strong but socially trusted.

7.2 Measuring and Improving Incident Readiness: Turning Metrics Into Actionable Insights for Product Teams

Resilience is not only about having plans and processes; it is about ensuring those plans work when tested. Measurement is therefore the backbone of readiness. Without metrics, organizations cannot know whether their incident management and continuity plans are effective or whether they exist only on paper.

Two common metrics; Recovery Time Objective (RTO) and Recovery Point Objective (RPO), are foundational. RTO measures how quickly systems must be restored after disruption, while RPO measures how much data loss is acceptable. A bank may set an RTO of one hour for its transaction services and an RPO of five minutes for customer data. These metrics provide clarity and align teams around specific performance goals. For product managers, understanding and championing these numbers ensures that customer expectations match technical capabilities.

But measurement should go further. How many incidents are detected internally before customers report them? How often are playbooks rehearsed? How long does it take to escalate incidents to decision-makers? These metrics reveal whether resilience is theoretical or operational. A Nigerian e-commerce company that conducted regular simulations discovered that while its engineers could restore systems quickly, customer communication lagged by hours. By measuring and addressing this gap, the company improved overall readiness.

Continuous improvement requires turning these insights into action. Post-mortems should not only identify technical fixes but also update playbooks, retrain teams, and refine metrics. Over time, measurement builds a culture of accountability. Teams know they will be evaluated not only on how often incidents occur but on how effectively they respond.

Product managers play a critical role in ensuring metrics are meaningful. They must translate technical indicators into business impacts showing leadership how downtime affects revenue, how communication delays affect churn, and how resilience improvements enhance customer loyalty. By grounding metrics in business value, PMs secure ongoing investment in resilience initiatives.

Ultimately, measurement transforms incident management from reactive firefighting into proactive preparation. It ensures that continuity planning is not static but dynamic, evolving with threats, technologies, and customer expectations. For product managers, driving this measurement culture is one of the most powerful ways to turn resilience into a sustained advantage.

Chapter 8

Cross-Functional Collaboration for Security Success

Resilience is never the achievement of a single team. It cannot be built by engineers working in isolation, nor can compliance officers, designers, or executives ensure it alone. Cyber-resilience emerges from the intersection of disciplines, from the cooperation of teams with different skills, incentives, and perspectives. For product managers, this reality creates both a challenge and an opportunity. The challenge lies in uniting groups that often operate in silos, with competing priorities and limited communication. The opportunity lies in transforming these silos into a network of collaboration that strengthens resilience across the entire product lifecycle.

Cross-functional collaboration means that security becomes everyone's responsibility, not just the domain of security specialists. It requires engineers to think about usability, designers to consider privacy, marketers to plan for crisis communication, and executives to fund resilience initiatives even when the returns are not immediate. Without this shared responsibility, gaps inevitably appear. A designer may build a feature that unintentionally exposes sensitive data. An engineer may harden infrastructure but neglect to make security features user-friendly. A marketing team may promote product claims that cannot be upheld during a breach. Product managers must bridge these divides, ensuring that resilience is not fragmented but holistic.

At the core of collaboration is communication. Teams cannot work together effectively if they do not understand one another's priorities. Security engineers may speak in technical jargon, designers in terms of flows, executives in terms of risk and revenue. The product manager's role is to act as translator, turning technical risks into business impacts, converting compliance requirements into customer value propositions, and reframing resilience not as an obstacle but as an enabler. When communication succeeds, collaboration flourishes.

Examples from Nigerian companies highlight both the pitfalls and the possibilities. A fintech startup once launched a new feature allowing merchants to onboard customers quickly. Engineering prioritized speed, design focused on simplicity, but compliance was left out of the loop. Within weeks, regulators flagged the feature for failing to meet Know Your Customer (KYC) requirements. The rollout had to be halted, costing time and reputation. By contrast, another startup in the same space created cross-functional squads where compliance officers, designers, and engineers worked together during feature planning. The result was slower initial development but faster approval, fewer redesigns, and stronger customer trust.

Collaboration also requires clarity of ownership. In many incidents, confusion arises not because teams are unwilling to help but because no one knows who is responsible. A resilient culture defines roles clearly: who monitors systems, who drafts communication, who approves escalations, who interacts with regulators. Product managers must document and socialize these roles, reducing ambiguity when crises occur.

Globally, some of the most resilient organizations such as Netflix, embed cross-functional collaboration into their DNA. Netflix's famed "Chaos Engineering" involves deliberately introducing failures into systems to test resilience. But the practice is not confined to engineers. Product managers, designers, and even customer support participate in simulations, ensuring that resilience is tested end-to-end. This holistic approach ensures that when real failures occur, the entire organization, not just one team is ready.

For collaboration to succeed, incentives must also be aligned. Engineers rewarded only for shipping features may see resilience as a distraction. Marketing teams measured only by growth metrics may downplay transparency during crises. Executives focused solely on quarterly revenue may resist resilience investments. Product managers must therefore work with leadership to align incentives, tying resilience to performance reviews, celebrating successful incident responses, and showcasing how resilience strengthens long-term growth.

8.1 Why Resilience Demands Shared Goals, Shared Language, and Shared Ownership

One of the greatest barriers to collaboration is the persistence of silos within organizations. Silos are not inherently malicious; they often emerge as teams specialize and focus on their domains. But when resilience is concerned, silos become dangerous. Attackers exploit the gaps between teams, where no one feels accountable.

Breaking silos begins with shared goals. If each team defines success differently; engineering as speed, compliance as adherence, marketing as growth, collaboration suffers. Product managers must establish resilience as a shared goal across functions. This does not mean abandoning other priorities but ensuring that security and continuity are recognized as part of everyone's definition of success. A Nigerian logistics startup achieved this by making "trust score" a key performance indicator across all teams. Engineers tracked uptime, designers tracked error rates, marketers tracked customer trust surveys, and compliance tracked regulatory performance. By uniting around trust, silos weakened and collaboration strengthened.

Shared language is equally important. When security engineers speak of "zero trust architectures" or "token mismanagement," designers or marketers may feel excluded. Conversely, when marketers speak of "brand perception," engineers may dismiss it as soft. Product managers must bridge these vocabularies, creating common terms that everyone can relate to. For example, framing resilience as "customer trust" translates across teams, while metrics like downtime in hours or customer complaints are universally understood.

Shared ownership is the final step. Teams must see resilience as something they co-own, not something handed to another department. This requires cultural change. When a failure occurs, the instinct should not be to point fingers but to ask, "how did our shared system allow this?" Product managers must model this behavior, celebrating cross-functional successes and reframing failures as collective learning opportunities.

Another dimension often overlooked is collaboration beyond the boundaries of the organization itself. In today's interconnected economy, no product exists in isolation. Vendors, regulators, industry associations, and even user communities play critical roles in resilience. Ignoring these relationships weakens resilience; nurturing them strengthens it.

Vendors provide essential services; cloud infrastructure, payment gateways, analytics tools that form part of the product's architecture. Product managers must build collaborative relationships with vendors, ensuring clear service-level agreements, transparent incident communication, and joint resilience drills. A Nigerian fintech once faced a crisis when its cloud provider suffered an outage. Because there was no structured collaboration, the fintech struggled to obtain updates, worsening customer frustration. A competitor that had established vendor communication protocols fared better, restoring trust more quickly.

Regulators, often seen as adversaries, can also be collaborators. Early engagement with regulators allows organizations to shape policies, anticipate changes, and secure goodwill. For instance, Nigerian fintech companies that participated in Central Bank consultations were better prepared for regulatory shifts than those who ignored the dialogue. Product managers must therefore advocate for proactive engagement, positioning the product as a responsible player in the ecosystem.

Communities, whether industry groups, open-source contributors, or even users are also powerful collaborators. Sharing information about emerging threats, learning from peers, and participating in collective security initiatives elevate resilience. Globally, organizations participate in Information Sharing and Analysis Centers (ISACs) that provide intelligence on sector-specific threats. Nigerian startups are beginning to form similar clusters, recognizing that resilience is stronger when knowledge is shared.

For product managers, collaboration beyond the organization means broadening their scope of responsibility. Resilience is not only about internal alignment but about positioning the product within an ecosystem of shared security. By forging external partnerships, PMs extend resilience beyond their walls, making their products harder to isolate and attack.

8.2 The Role of Leadership in Driving Cross-Functional Security Collaboration

Collaboration across functions does not arise spontaneously. It requires leadership to set the tone, allocate resources, and model accountability. In many organizations, product managers find themselves in the middle, trying to unite teams that are technically willing but structurally constrained. Leadership support can be the difference between cross-functional collaboration that thrives and one that collapses under competing priorities.

Executives play a critical role by framing security and resilience not as departmental concerns but as strategic imperatives. When CEOs and CTOs publicly emphasize that security is a board-level priority, teams across functions take notice. Conversely, when leaders focus exclusively on speed or growth, other priorities overshadow resilience. For example, a Nigerian startup that treated resilience as "non-revenue work" consistently underfunded security initiatives. Eventually, a high-profile breach forced leadership to invest reactively at far higher cost than proactive investment would have required.

Resource allocation is another leadership function. Collaboration demands time for joint workshops, budget for resilience tools, and training for staff across functions. Without these resources, collaboration becomes aspirational rather than practical. Leaders must ensure that resilience is funded as deliberately as marketing campaigns or feature rollouts.

Finally, leadership must model accountability. When incidents occur, leaders who blame teams discourage transparency, making future collaboration weaker. Leaders who take responsibility, support their teams, and drive collective learning foster trust across functions. Product managers should advocate for this model, reminding leadership that resilience is an organizational responsibility, not an individual failure.

8.3 From Collaboration to Culture: Embedding Security Mindsets Into Everyday Product Practices

Collaboration achieves little if it is limited to meetings, workshops, or crisis moments. To truly succeed, it must evolve into culture, a set of shared behaviors and assumptions that guide everyday work. Culture ensures that resilience does not depend on the presence of particular individuals but becomes part of "how we do things here."

Embedding security into culture begins with daily rituals. If standups include quick mentions of potential risks, teams internalize risk awareness as natural. If retrospectives discuss not only what went well but also what resilience gaps were exposed, security becomes part of continuous improvement. If designers ask, "how might this feature be abused?" during ideation sessions, security considerations enter creativity rather than oppose it.

Cultural reinforcement also comes through recognition. When teams successfully collaborate to prevent an incident, their work should be celebrated as much as launching a new feature. When resilience saves the organization from disruption, leadership should highlight it as a win, not treat it as invisible. Over time, these signals shift perceptions: resilience stops being the "invisible work" and becomes a recognized part of product success.

Examples abound. A Nigerian healthtech startup introduced a cultural practice called "Friday Security Check-ins," where engineers, designers, and compliance officers discussed one resilience topic weekly in a short session. This lightweight ritual created ongoing awareness and encouraged informal collaboration. Globally, companies like Microsoft run "security awareness months" that gamify learning across departments, embedding resilience into corporate identity.

For product managers, embedding culture means consistently reinforcing the message that resilience is not separate from innovation—it is part of innovation. When security mindsets are woven into everyday practices, collaboration becomes second nature. Teams stop asking, "Who is responsible for security?" and start saying, "Security is something we all own."

Chapter 9

Measuring Cyber-Resilience and Communicating Value

"You cannot improve what you do not measure." This timeless principle applies as much to cyber-resilience as it does to revenue or customer engagement. For product managers, resilience cannot remain an abstract ideal. It must be translated into measurable outcomes that can be tracked, improved, and communicated to stakeholders. Without measurement, resilience initiatives risk being dismissed as costs without clear returns. Without communication, their value may be invisible to leadership, investors, and customers.

Measuring cyber-resilience is complex because it spans multiple dimensions: technical performance, human readiness, regulatory compliance, and customer trust. Each of these must be quantified in ways that are meaningful to both technical teams and business leaders. For example, measuring mean time to detect (MTTD) and mean time to respond (MTTR) provides insight into operational readiness, while tracking customer churn after an incident reveals resilience's impact on trust. Product managers must learn to bridge these dimensions, ensuring that resilience metrics align with overall business goals.

Frameworks such as the NIST Cybersecurity Framework and ISO 27001 provide structured approaches to resilience measurement. They outline categories such as identify, protect, detect, respond, and recover, helping teams ensure that no area is overlooked. For product managers, these frameworks provide language that resonates with regulators and investors, signaling maturity and credibility. But frameworks must be adapted to local realities. Nigerian startups, for instance, may not have the resources for full ISO certification but can still adopt lightweight practices such as periodic audits, incident drills, and customer surveys.

Communicating value is as important as measuring it. Too often, resilience metrics are trapped in technical dashboards that never reach decision-makers. Executives care less about the number of vulnerabilities patched than about the business risk reduced. Customers care less about server uptimes than about uninterrupted access to services. Investors care less about compliance certificates than about confidence that the product will not collapse under pressure. Product managers must translate resilience outcomes into these terms, telling stories that connect technical measures to human and financial impact.

One of the biggest obstacles product managers faces is the perception that resilience does not generate revenue. Sales teams bring in customers, marketing drives visibility, engineering builds features—but resilience seems invisible. Until a crisis hits. Then, suddenly, everyone realizes its value. The challenge is to make that value visible before disaster strikes.

Measuring resilience provides the evidence needed to make the business case. Metrics such as reduced downtime, faster incident response, and lower customer churn demonstrate tangible returns. For example, if a continuity feature prevents 10,000 failed transactions during a system outage, that is not just resilience it is revenue preserved. If improved communication during incidents reduces customer complaints by 40 percent, that is not just PR—it is brand loyalty protected.

Product managers must frame resilience as return on investment (ROI). This involves quantifying not only direct financial impacts but also indirect ones such as regulatory goodwill, investor confidence, and market differentiation. A startup that can demonstrate resilience maturity may attract more cautious enterprise clients, opening markets that competitors cannot access. In this way, resilience is not only about avoiding loss but about enabling growth.

Numbers alone rarely inspire action. Stakeholders respond to stories narratives that connect metrics to human experience. Product managers must therefore become storytellers of resilience, using data as raw material for narratives that highlight the stakes and the successes.

A story might begin with a customer who avoided financial loss because continuity systems rerouted their transaction. It might describe how a startup survived a regional power outage because of redundant infrastructure. It might showcase how a healthcare app earned patient trust by being transparent about incident response. These stories translate abstract metrics into concrete outcomes that resonate with customers, regulators, and investors.

Storytelling also involves transparency about failures. A company that admits to an incident, explains what went wrong, and demonstrates what was learned gains credibility. Silence or denial, by contrast, destroys trust. By framing incidents as opportunities for growth, product managers turn setbacks into demonstrations of resilience.

Another often overlooked area is the forward-looking dimension of measurement. Resilience metrics cannot remain static because threats evolve, technologies shift, and customer expectations rise. What is considered resilient today may be fragile tomorrow.

For example, five years ago, few companies measured resilience against supply chain attacks. Today, such metrics are essential as attackers increasingly target vendors. Similarly, resilience metrics once focused on system availability alone. Now, privacy breaches, misinformation campaigns, and AI-driven attacks require broader measurement. Product managers must anticipate these shifts, updating metrics to reflect emerging risks.

Future expectations will also shape measurement. Customers may soon demand real-time visibility into system health. Regulators may require standardized resilience disclosures. Investors may expect quantified resilience maturity scores before funding. By preparing for this evolution, product managers position their products ahead of the curve.

In Nigeria, as digital adoption accelerates, resilience measurement will likely expand to include national security dimensions. Products that can demonstrate resilience not only protect their users but also contribute to economic stability. By adopting forward-looking metrics, PMs ensure their products remain credible and competitive in both local and global markets.

9.1 Measuring Human Resilience: Why Team Readiness and Culture Are as Important as Technical Metrics

Cyber-resilience is often measured in purely technical terms; uptime, detection rates, patch cycles. Yet, incidents rarely remain confined to technology. Human response determines whether technical safeguards succeed or fail. If teams panic, delay communication, or make poor decisions under stress, even the strongest systems may crumble. Measuring human resilience is therefore just as important as monitoring servers or networks.

Human resilience can be assessed through incident response drills. How quickly do teams escalate an issue? Do they follow the playbook or improvise chaotically? Are communication channels clear, or do silos cause confusion? These drills should not be theoretical exercises but simulations that mimic real-world stress. Nigerian banks have begun running “fire drills” for cyberattacks, measuring how employees across departments respond to simulated breaches. The results often reveal more about resilience than technical dashboards.

Another way to measure human resilience is through surveys and cultural audits. Do employees feel empowered to report risks? Do they believe leadership values security, or do they feel pressured to cut corners? If staff fear punishment for mistakes, incidents may go unreported until it is too late. By measuring culture through anonymous feedback, participation in training, or the frequency of reported near-misses product managers gain insights into resilience that numbers alone cannot capture.

Finally, leadership behavior must be measured. How often do executives attend resilience reviews? Do they allocate budgets proactively, or only after crises? If leadership does not have a model commitment, resilience initiatives remain fragile. Measuring human readiness, therefore, means evaluating not only frontline staff but the entire organizational hierarchy. For product managers, weaving these assessments into resilience reporting ensures that the human dimension is visible, valued, and continually improved.

9.2 Communicating Resilience to External Stakeholders: Building Confidence With Customers, Regulators, and Investors

Measurement achieves little if it is kept hidden inside internal dashboards. The real power of resilience lies in its communication, sharing achievements, acknowledging risks, and signaling credibility to external stakeholders. Customers, regulators, and investors all look for signs that a product can withstand disruption, and product managers must shape the narratives that convey this assurance.

For customers, communication must focus on **trust and usability**. A Nigerian fintech might highlight its 99.95 percent transaction uptime, not as a raw number but as "your payments will go through even during peak demand." Similarly, a healthtech platform might emphasize compliance with the Nigeria Data Protection Act, framed as "your medical records are safe and private." Customers care about outcomes, not frameworks, so communication must translate resilience into benefits they experience.

For regulators, communication must emphasize **compliance and transparency**. Regulators do not expect perfection, but they demand accountability. Proactively sharing audit outcomes, incident reports, and remediation efforts builds credibility. In fact, organizations that engage openly with regulators often receive more favorable treatment during crises. Product managers can champion this approach by ensuring compliance results are not hidden but presented confidently as evidence of maturity.

For investors, communication must highlight **resilience as a growth enabler**. Investors want assurance that products can scale without collapsing and that crises will not erase value. By presenting resilience metrics in financial terms such as revenue preserved during outages, regulatory fines avoided, or new markets unlocked through compliance; PMs frame resilience as return on investment. This narrative reassures investors that resilience is not a defensive cost but a strategic asset.

Ultimately, communication is about balance. Overstating resilience creates false confidence and risk of backlash during incidents. Understating it leaves value hidden. Product managers must strike a tone of pragmatic confidence, acknowledging challenges honestly, while demonstrating the systems, culture, and metrics in place to address them. When done well, this communication transforms resilience from an invisible shield into a visible source of trust.

Chapter 10

The Future of Cyber-Resilient Product Management

The digital world is in constant motion. Technologies advance, threats evolve, and customer expectations shift. What we consider cyber-resilient today may look outdated tomorrow. For product managers, this creates both risk and opportunity. Risk, because ignoring the future means building products that quickly become fragile. Opportunity, because anticipating trends allows PMs to design products that are not only secure but future-proof, giving them a decisive edge in competitive markets.

The future of cyber-resilient product management will be defined by three converging forces: the rise of artificial intelligence (AI) and automation, the increasing complexity of global regulatory landscapes, and the growing centrality of trust as a differentiator in markets. Each of these forces requires new thinking, new tools, and new leadership from product managers.

AI will shape both the threats and the defenses of tomorrow. Attackers are already using machine learning to automate phishing campaigns, bypass security measures, and discover vulnerabilities faster than humans can patch them. But AI also offers defenders powerful tools—threat detection systems that learn patterns of attack, fraud monitoring algorithms that adapt to new behaviors, and automated responses that contain incidents in real time. For product managers, the challenge will be integrating AI into products responsibly. This means not only leveraging AI for resilience but also ensuring AI systems themselves are resilient against manipulation, bias, and abuse.

Regulatory complexity will also intensify. As digital products cross borders more easily than ever before, they will encounter overlapping and sometimes conflicting regulations. A fintech operating in Nigeria, Kenya, and Europe may face three different data protection regimes, each with unique requirements. The future will demand architectures flexible enough to adapt to multiple compliance contexts without costly redesigns. Product managers must anticipate this complexity, building governance frameworks that scale across geographies.

Finally, trust will become the currency of digital products. In an age of deepfakes, misinformation, and data breaches, customers will increasingly choose products not only for features or price but for credibility. Products that can prove they are resilient, transparent, and accountable will win loyalty. For product managers, this elevates resilience from a technical or regulatory concern to a central part of the value proposition. Tomorrow's competitive advantage will not belong to the fastest mover but to the most trusted partner.

Every new technology creates both opportunities and risks for resilience. Cloud computing, once seen as a radical shift, is now standard—but it has introduced risks of misconfiguration and dependency on external providers. The next wave of technologies will be no different.

Blockchain, for example, offers decentralized trust mechanisms that could make systems harder to tamper with. Yet, blockchain also raises resilience challenges such as scalability issues, energy demands, and governance disputes. Internet of Things (IoT) devices expand connectivity but multiply attack surfaces, creating vulnerabilities at the edge. Quantum computing, still emerging, promises breakthroughs in processing power but threatens to break existing encryption standards, forcing a rethink of security fundamentals.

Product managers must approach new technologies with **balanced optimism**. They must ask: How does this technology enhance resilience? How does it threaten it? How can we design safeguards before adoption becomes widespread? In Nigeria, where mobile-first innovations often leapfrog traditional infrastructure, this balanced approach is critical. For instance, mobile money has expanded financial access but also created new fraud vectors. Anticipating these dualities allows PMs to lead adoption responsibly.

10.1 The Evolving Role of the Product Manager in Cyber-Resilience

As resilience becomes central to product success, the role of the product manager will expand. No longer will PMs be seen solely as coordinators of features and timelines. They will increasingly act as **stewards of trust**, responsible for ensuring that products deliver safety as reliably as they deliver functionality.

This expanded role requires new skills. PMs must become conversant in security principles, regulatory frameworks, and risk management strategies. They need not be security engineers or compliance officers, but they must understand enough to ask the right questions, challenge assumptions, and align stakeholders. They must also become skilled communicators, able to tell compelling stories about resilience that resonate with executives, investors, and customers.

In practice, this means PMs will lead conversations about resilience in strategy meetings, shape budgets for resilience initiatives, and advocate for resilience as part of product value. It also means they will navigate tensions between speed and security, short-term gains and long-term sustainability. The PM of the future is not only a builder of features but a builder of trust ecosystems.

Cyber-resilience cannot be divorced from broader global forces. Geopolitical tensions increasingly spill into cyberspace, with state-sponsored attacks targeting companies as proxies. Products operating in multiple regions may become entangled in conflicts beyond their control. Nigerian fintechs serving diaspora communities, for instance, may face risks from international sanctions, cross-border data restrictions, or politically motivated cyber campaigns.

Climate change also intersects with resilience. Extreme weather events disrupt data centers, power grids, and supply chains. Products that rely on fragile infrastructure may falter as floods, heatwaves, or storms intensify. Continuity planning must therefore expand beyond digital threats to physical vulnerabilities. Product managers for the future must ask: How does climate risk affect our infrastructure? How can we ensure continuity when both digital and physical systems are stressed?

Societal change will also shape resilience. As digital literacy expands, customers will demand greater transparency and control. At the same time, social inequalities may create uneven resilience, urban areas enjoying robust connectivity while rural areas remain fragile. PMs must design products that bridge these divides, ensuring resilience is inclusive rather than exclusive. By anticipating these global shifts, PMs can position their products not just to survive but to lead in uncertain futures.

The future of resilience will not be built by individual companies acting alone. Threats are too fast, too global, and too complex for isolation. Instead, shared resilience, collaboration across borders, industries, and communities will define the next era.

Industry collaboration is already growing through information-sharing groups and joint defense initiatives. Tech companies share threat intelligence to stop attacks before they spread. Financial institutions collaborate on fraud detection systems that pool data across competitors. These collective approaches turn resilience into a shared resource. Nigerian startups can benefit by joining regional and global alliances, ensuring they are not isolated when threats emerge.

Cross-border collaboration will also be essential. Cybercrime knows no borders, and neither can resilience. Products serving African markets must work with regulators and partners across countries, building interoperable frameworks for security and compliance. International partnerships not only strengthen defenses but also open opportunities for expansion.

Community collaboration is equally important. Users themselves must be part of resilience ecosystems, reporting threats, adopting safe behaviors, and supporting transparent communication. The future PM will see customers not as passive recipients of protection but as active participants in resilience.

By building a future of shared resilience, product managers help create ecosystems where threats are less likely to succeed, trust is more widely distributed, and innovation can flourish without constant fear of collapse.

10.2 Case Study 1: A Nigerian Fintech's AI Gamble, Balancing Innovation With Resilience

In 2027, a fast-rising Nigerian fintech startup, let's call it **PayNova**, decided to integrate artificial intelligence into its fraud detection system. The promise was enormous: AI models could scan millions of transactions in real time, detecting patterns of fraud that human analysts might miss. Investors hailed the move as a leap into the future, and PayNova positioned itself as a pioneer in AI-driven security.

At first, the results were impressive. Fraudulent transactions dropped by 40 percent, customer trust grew, and partnerships with banks flourished. But within a year, attackers adapted. By studying how the AI system flagged fraud, they began training adversarial models designed to fool PayNova's detection algorithms. Transactions that looked legitimate but concealed fraud began slipping through. Customers who had once praised PayNova now accused it of overconfidence.

The turning point came during a major cyberattack in 2028, when coordinated adversarial inputs bypassed the AI system, causing millions in losses. PayNova's credibility plummeted, and regulators demanded answers.

The lesson for product managers was clear: AI cannot be treated as a silver bullet. Resilience requires layered defenses. PayNova eventually rebuilt its system, combining AI with human oversight, stronger governance, and transparent communication with users. What started as a near-disaster evolved into a recovery story, but only because leadership admitted mistakes and invested in broader resilience strategies.

For future PMs, PayNova's case illustrates the dual edge of emerging technologies: they create competitive advantage, but they also introduce new attack surfaces. Building for resilience means not only adopting innovations but anticipating how adversaries will adapt to them.

10.3 Case Study 2: A Global HealthTech Platform's Continuity Challenge Designing for Climate and Connectivity Risks

While cyberattacks dominate headlines, physical realities also test resilience. In 2029, **MediLink**, a global healthtech platform serving clinics in Africa, Asia, and Latin America, faced a crisis when extreme weather struck multiple regions simultaneously. Floods in Lagos disrupted data centers, while heatwaves in India triggered rolling blackouts. MediLink's cloud-based architecture was theoretically redundant, but because most of its backup nodes were concentrated in Europe, latency soared, and some services failed entirely.

Clinics depending on MediLink for patient records suddenly found themselves locked out. Doctors in Nigerian rural areas, already struggling with unreliable connectivity, faced chaos as patients arrived without access to digital histories. Social media amplified the frustration, with patients accusing MediLink of neglecting the realities of developing markets.

The incident forced MediLink to rethink continuity planning. Instead of assuming global redundancy was enough, the company began designing **regional resilience strategies**: smaller, distributed data centers in Africa and Asia, offline-first functionality for clinics in low-connectivity zones, and solar-powered edge servers for areas vulnerable to grid failures.

Within two years, MediLink not only restored its reputation but became a case study in inclusive resilience. By acknowledging that continuity must account for climate, geography, and socio-economic contexts, it turned resilience into a market advantage. Clinics that once doubted digital systems embraced MediLink precisely because it proved adaptable to their realities.

For product managers, MediLink's case underscores a critical insight: the future of resilience extends beyond digital threats. Physical risks, from climate to infrastructure must be integrated into continuity planning. Products that anticipate these realities will not only survive crises but also lead markets hungry for dependable solutions.

Reviews

1. Chinedu Okafor, Cybersecurity Analyst, Lagos

A Product Manager's Guide to Building Cyber-Resilient Products is a book that speaks directly to the realities we face in the Nigerian tech space. Too often, product managers leave security to the IT team, but Adebayo shows that resilience begins with leadership at the product level. His practical insights on collaboration and governance make this a valuable tool not only for PMs but for anyone working on digital platforms. Reading this book gave me new ways to communicate risks to business leaders and to push for stronger security practices in my organization.

2. Halima Danjuma, Entrepreneur and Founder of a Fintech Startup, Abuja

As someone building financial products in Nigeria, I know how devastating a single breach can be for customer trust. This book explains resilience in a way that is not intimidating but very practical. What impressed me most is how Adebayo balances the global standards of resilience with examples that reflect African realities. For startups like mine, this book is a survival guide. It should be required reading for every founder and product team.

3. *Tunde Akinyemi, Lecturer in Information Systems, University of Ibadan*

This work fills an important gap in product management education. While many books focus on features and design, few deal with resilience in such a comprehensive manner. Adebayo Kalejaiye provides frameworks that students, researchers, and professionals can apply immediately. His chapter on governance and compliance is particularly valuable, especially in helping Nigerian businesses align with global expectations. I will be recommending this book to my postgraduate students as a reference text.

4. *Ifeoma Nwachukwu, Senior Product Manager, Telecommunications Industry, Lagos*

In the telecom sector, where millions of customers depend on reliable services every day, resilience is everything. I found Adebayo's book refreshing because it goes beyond buzzwords to show the real responsibilities of product managers in ensuring security and continuity. His emphasis on cross-functional collaboration resonates with me, since resilience is never achieved in isolation. This book is one of the most practical resources I have seen in years, and I know it will shape how many PMs approach their roles.

5. *Musa Abdullahi, Policy Advisor on Digital Economy, Kano*

The digital economy cannot thrive without resilient products. Governments, businesses, and communities are all affected when systems fail. This book is important because it speaks to product managers as leaders who must anticipate risks, not just respond to them. Adebayo has written a text that bridges policy, technology, and management. It is rare to see a Nigerian voice contribute so powerfully to this global conversation. I strongly recommend this book to anyone working at the intersection of technology and society..

References

Alhassan, I., Sammon, D., & Daly, M. (2018). Data governance activities: An analysis of the literature. *Journal of Decision Systems, 27*(sup1), 64–81. https://doi.org/10.1080/12460125.2018.1468697

Böhme, R., Laube, S., & Riek, M. (2020). A fundamental approach to cyber risk analysis. *Economics of Information Security and Privacy*, 1–31. Springer. https://doi.org/10.1007/978-3-030-42525-4_1

Central Bank of Nigeria. (2023). *Risk-based cybersecurity framework and guidelines for other financial institutions.* Abuja: CBN. Retrieved from https://www.cbn.gov.ng

Cybersecurity and Infrastructure Security Agency. (2022). *Cyber resilience review (CRR) resource guide.* U.S. Department of Homeland Security. https://www.cisa.gov

International Organization for Standardization. (2018). *ISO/IEC 27001:2018 – Information security management systems.* Geneva: ISO.

National Institute of Standards and Technology. (2018). *Framework for improving critical infrastructure cybersecurity (Version 1.1).* Gaithersburg, MD: U.S. Department of Commerce. https://doi.org/10.6028/NIST.CSWP.04162018

Nigeria Data Protection Bureau. (2023). *Nigeria Data Protection Act.* Abuja: NDPB. Retrieved from https://ndpb.gov.ng

PwC Nigeria. (2021). *The future of cybersecurity in Nigeria: Building trust in the digital economy.* Lagos: PricewaterhouseCoopers Nigeria. Retrieved from https://www.pwc.com/ng

Renaud, K., & Flowerday, S. (2017). Contemplating human-centered security & privacy research: Suggesting future directions. *Journal of Information Security and Applications, 34,* 76–84. https://doi.org/10.1016/j.jisa.2016.06.002

Shackleford, D. (2019). Building a practical security program. *SANS Institute InfoSec Reading Room.* Retrieved from https://www.sans.org

Soomro, Z. A., Shah, M. H., & Ahmed, J. (2016). Information security management needs more holistic approach: A literature review. *International Journal of Information Management, 36*(2), 215–225. https://doi.org/10.1016/j.ijinfomgt.2015.11.009

World Economic Forum. (2022). *Global cybersecurity outlook 2022.* Geneva: WEF. Retrieved from https://www.weforum.org